Staying Safe

Dr. Alvin Silverstein,

Virginia Silverstein, and

Laura Silverstein Nunn

My Health

Franklin Watts

A Division of Grolier Publishing

New York • London • Hong Kong • Sydney

Danbury, Connecticut

Photographs©: Corbis-Bettmann: 9; Craig D. Wood: 12; Custom Medical Stock Photo: 7; Nance S. Trueworthy: 15, 40; Photo Researchers: 18 (Tim Davis), 31 (Ellen B. Senisi); PhotoEdit: 39 (Laura Dwight), 20, 36 (M. Ferguson), 4, 23 bottom (Tony Freeman), 14, 28 (Michael Newman), 30 (James Shaffer), 33 (Rhoda Sidney), 16, 21, 25, 41 (D. Young-Wolff); Stock Boston: 11 (John Coletti), 34 (Billy E. Barnes), 13, 32 (Bob Daemmrich), 26 (Lawrence Migdale); Superstock, Inc.: 10, 17; The Image Works: 23 top (Bob Daemmrich); Tony Stone Images: 29 (Donald Johnston), 35 (Camille Tokerud); Unicorn Stock Photos: 8 (Jim Shippee); Visuals Unlimited: 19 (Rob & Ann Simpson).

Cartoons by Rick Stromoski

Visit Franklin Watts on the Internet at:
http://publishing.grolier.com

Library of Congress Cataloging-in-Publication Data

Silverstein, Alvin.
    Staying safe / by Alvin Silverstein, Virginia Silverstein, and Laura Silverstein Nunn.
        p.   cm.—(My Health)
    Includes bibliographical references and index.
    Summary: Describes potential dangers at home, at play, on streets and roads, at school, and when interacting with other people and explains what to do in an emergency.
    ISBN 0-531-11639-5 (lib. bdg.)   0-531-16509-4 (pbk.)
    1. Accidents—Prevention—Juvenile literature. 2. Children's accidents—Prevention—Juvenile literature. 3. Safety education—Juvenile literature. [1. Safety.] I. Silverstein, Virginia B. II. Nunn, Laura Silverstein. III. Title. IV. Series.
HV675.5.S55   2000
613.6—dc21   99-049662

GROLIER
PUBLISHING

Contents

Dangers All Around

We all face dangers every day. But luckily, it's not too hard to stay safe and still have fun. If you know about the dangers around you, you can prevent most accidents. That means you can stop them before they happen.

That's why your parents say things like: "Don't jump on the bed!" "Don't swing too high on the swings at the playground!" "Don't play with matches!" "Don't talk to strangers!" and "Look both ways before you cross the street!" All these warnings might bug you, but your parents are just trying to keep you safe.

Safety is all about knowing how to avoid danger and learning what to do if an accident does happen. The more you know, the safer you will be, so read on.

◀ How high is too high? You don't want to find out.

Did You Know...

Every year, millions of children have accidents that require medical attention. More children die from accidents than from illnesses.

Safety at Home

"Hot! Don't touch!" This is one of the first warnings that most kids hear—but they don't always listen. Touching a hot stove, an iron, or a radiator can cause a really painful burn. Some burns are mild, but others are quite serious. Even a mild burn can really hurt. If you ever need to touch something hot, remember to wear fireproof oven mitts.

Among the most common household accidents are falls—especially in the bathroom. When you take a bath or shower, the floor may get wet and slippery. You are less likely to slip and fall if you step onto a sturdy rug or towel when you get out of the bathtub or shower. Sometimes people slip while they are still in the bathtub. Placing a nonskid mat or adhesive strips on the bottom of the tub will make it safer.

Did You Know...

People used to put butter on burns, but it does not help. In fact, it may make the injury worse. If you get a burn, you should run cold water over it right away. Cold water soothes the pain and keeps the burn from blistering.

People fall in other parts of the house too. If you leave toys, games, or clothes on the floor or on the stairs, you—or someone else—could trip and get hurt. It is important to put your things away.

Knives are not toys! If a knife can slice through a loaf of bread, think about what it can do to your finger. Be very careful with knives and other sharp objects. Never run while carrying a knife, a pair of scissors, nails, a pencil, or other sharp objects.

A knife can be a useful tool if you handle it properly.

You should never fool around with **electricity**. If someone dares you to stick your finger into an electrical outlet, don't do it! Electricity can be very dangerous. That's easy to forget because you use it every day. You use it when you watch TV, vacuum the carpet, and make toast.

We need electricity to make toasters and other appliances work, but it's important to remember that it can be dangerous.

If you stick anything into an electrical outlet, an **electric current** will go through your body and give you an electric shock. A weak shock feels like a tingle. A strong shock feels like a punch.

Did you ever walk across a carpet and then get a shock when you touched a doorknob or another person? The shock you would get from an electrical outlet is a lot stronger than that. It can burn you, knock you out, or even kill you.

Careful Kite Flying

Hundreds of years ago, a man named Benjamin Franklin wanted to prove that lightning is produced by electricity. He decided to experiment by flying a kite in a thunderstorm. When a lightning bolt hit his kite, electric current flowed down the string to a metal key he had tied to the end. Franklin was lucky that he only felt a tingling in his fingers. Two people who tried to repeat his experiment were killed! We can all learn from history. If you're flying a kite, stay away from power lines—and thunderstorms.

In his famous kite experiment, Benjamin Franklin proved that lightning is a form of electricity.

Keep all electrical equipment away from water. Don't use blow dryers, curling irons, radios, or any other electrical gadgets while running water in a sink or bathtub. Never touch anything electric while your hands are wet. Electricity and water are a dangerous combination.

Do you have an octopus in your living room? Many people do. They plug too many things—lamps, clocks, radios, TVs, vacuum cleaners, and computers—into the same outlet. The cords spread out like the tentacles of an octopus. This kind of octopus could start a fire.

Do you have an octopus in your home? Limit the number of plugs in a single outlet.

When too many electrical appliances are plugged into one outlet, an electrical **circuit** may get overloaded Soon it will start to heat up. Then a fire may break out.

Learn about fire safety so this won't happen to your home.

It is scary to think about your home burning down. You can help prevent fires by following these safety tips:

- Don't overload electrical outlets.
- Don't use appliances that spark, smell strange, or overheat.
- Don't play with matches or cigarette lighters.
- Don't leave papers, clothes, or other **flammable** objects near a lamp or a stove or a space heater.
- Don't leave candles burning when no one is in the room.

Fires Need to Breathe

You know you need oxygen to breathe, but did you know that a fire needs oxygen to burn? The best way to put out a fire is to cut off its oxygen supply. To stop an oil or grease fire on the stove, put a big lid over it. Never pour water on a grease or oil fire. The water could splash the grease around and spread the fire.

Got a grease fire?
Put a lid on it!

Fires can happen anytime, anywhere. You can help make sure your family is prepared for one. Keep the number of the fire department next to the phone, and keep fire extinguishers handy. Every adult should know how to operate one.

Check that there are smoke detectors throughout your home, especially near the bedrooms. Test each smoke detector once a month. Replace the batteries twice a year. (Think you'll forget? Make a habit of changing the batteries when you change your clocks in spring and fall.)

If you hear a smoke detector chirping, the battery is running low. If you hear the smoke alarm, leave the house immediately. Call the fire department from a neighbor's house. Smoke detectors can reduce the number of deaths in a home fire by as much as 50 percent.

Every home should have a working smoke detector on each floor.

Make sure you and your family know all the ways to get out of your house in a hurry. Upstairs bedrooms should have escape ladders outside the window. Have a plan for escaping from your home in case of a fire and then have family fire drills to practice your escape.

Does your family have a plan of escape in case of a fire?

When you practice escaping, crawl across the floor. Because smoke rises, it will be easier to breathe near the floor. Before you open a door, make sure it is not hot. If the doorknob is warm, it means the fire is close. Do not open the door. Exit through a window. Decide on a special meeting place outside for your family. Then you will know that everyone is safe. If your clothes catch on fire, remember to *stop*, *drop*, and *roll*.

Safety at Play

What do you like to do after school? Ride your bike or skateboard? Go rollerblading? Play baseball or soccer? If it's winter, maybe you like to go sledding or ice skating. Whatever you do, are you playing it safe?

Some kids like to be daring. Have you ever asked yourself, "How high can I go on the swings?" "How fast can I get across the monkey bars?" Have you ever tried going up the slide instead of down? These things may seem fun, but they can also be dangerous.

This skateboarder knows what it means to play it safe.

Swinging too high on a swing may lead to a nasty fall. Trying to cross the monkey bars too fast may result in some serious cuts and scrapes. Climbing up a slide is not a good idea, especially if someone else is on the way down. It is important to follow safety rules on the playground. Otherwise you could get hurt, or you could accidentally hurt someone else.

If possible, pick a playground with a soft surface, such as sawdust, wood chips, mulch, or sand. They help to cushion falls. You are more likely to get hurt on playgrounds with blacktop, dirt, or grass surfaces.

If you monkey around on the monkey bars, someone can get hurt.

Before you take off on your bike, skateboard, or rollerblades, put on a helmet! Are you afraid you might not look cool? Wearing a helmet is not only cool, it's smart. A helmet protects your brain. Cuts, bruises, and broken bones can heal, but head injuries may never get better. To protect yourself even more, wear knee pads, elbow pads, and wrist pads.

This roller-blader knows how to stay safe. She is wearing a helmet, knee pads, and wrist pads.

Heads Up!

Every year, thousands of kids get head injuries in bike accidents. Wearing a helmet reduces the risk of head injury by 85 percent. In some states, children under the age of 14 must wear helmets. It's the law!

Helmets and padding are also a good idea when you play team sports. Whenever kids are active, injuries can happen. Whether you are playing baseball, soccer, football, or hockey, protective gear is a must. When you play baseball, a helmet protects your head from wild pitches. Knee pads and elbow pads help keep you safe during a soccer game. Football players need helmets, shin guards, knee pads, shoulder pads, and elbow pads.

For many people, summer is a time for fun in the sun. What could be nicer

A helmet protects a batter from head injuries.

than a day at the beach? You should take along plenty of sunscreen or sunblock, though. The sun's powerful **ultraviolet rays** (UV rays) can give you a painful sunburn.

Sunburn is a warning that UV rays have hurt your skin. Even though the sunburn eventually goes away, the damage to the skin remains. Some studies show that kids who get sunburned a lot have a higher risk of getting skin cancer as adults.

Ouch! That hurts! Sunburn is a sign of damage to your skin.

Sunscreen soaks up some of the sun's UV rays, so they never get a chance to hurt your skin. Sunblock is even better. It keeps *all* of the UV rays from reaching your skin. When you put on sunscreen or sunblock, you are putting on an invisible suit of armor. The best sunscreens and sunblocks have a Sun Protection Factor (SPF) of 15 or higher. If you sweat a lot or go swimming, be sure to reapply these lotions.

Does Everybody Get Sunburned?

Anyone can get sunburned—no matter what color their skin is. However, people with light-colored skin burn more easily than people with dark-colored skin. Human skin contains tiny black grains called **melanin** that protect us from the sun's harmful rays. Dark skin contains more melanin than light skin, so it can handle more sun.

The ancestors of people with dark skin came from Africa, Central America, and other places where the sun is very bright and hot. The ancestors of people with very light skin came from Norway, Sweden, and other places where the sun is weaker.

Imagine yourself cruising along in a boat on a large, beautiful lake. Suddenly, the boat tips over and you are thrown into the water. What should you do? It is important to know some rules about water safety.

Never go out in a boat without putting on a life preserver. It is also a good idea to take a few swimming lessons. Everyone should know how to swim, float, and **tread water**. Floating and treading water are less tiring than swimming. You can stay afloat longer and improve your chances of being rescued.

A canoe ride can be fun (left), but before you head out, know what to do if you tip over. Learning how to float can keep you safe in the water (below).

23

Activity 1: Make Your Own Floats

Some people have saved themselves from drowning by using their pants, shirts, or jackets as floats. Try tying the bottoms of a pair of pants together and then swish them around to fill them with air before tying off the top. You have made a balloon that will float in the water and could help to hold you up. Test it in a bathtub to see how well it floats. Balls, plastic buckets, hats, and milk jugs can also be used as floats.

If a friend is in trouble in the swimming pool, don't jump in and try to save him or her. Call for help and try to find a float or pole for your friend to grab. If you tried to rescue the person yourself, your friend might panic and pull you under too.

Safety on Streets and Roads

Be sure to look both ways before you cross the street. Most kids learn this basic safety rule when they are very young—and it's a good one to remember. You don't

Look both ways before you cross the street.

always know how drivers will act. They may not see you. Even if they do see you, they may not have enough time to stop. It's up to you to look out for yourself.

Whether you are walking down the road, pedaling a bike, or just riding in a car, you need to learn the rules of the road.

Whenever possible, cross the street at an intersection or a crosswalk. Before you step off the curb, *stop*, *look* both ways, and *listen* for cars. Do not cross until you are sure that no cars are coming. If there is

Crosswalks make crossing the street safer.

Rules of the Road

Bike riders must use the right side of the street and travel in the same direction as cars. People who walk on the street must walk on the left side and travel in the opposite direction from cars. That way, the **pedestrians** can see the cars coming.

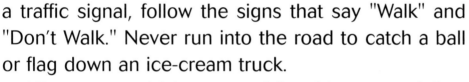

Many traffic accidents involving pedestrians occur between 4:00 P.M. and 8:00 P.M. Many children are walking home from school at this time, and many adults are driving home from work.

a traffic signal, follow the signs that say "Walk" and "Don't Walk." Never run into the road to catch a ball or flag down an ice-cream truck.

Like anyone driving a car, bike riders must follow safety rules too. Bike riders need to know the hand signals for a left turn, a right turn, and stop. Before making a left turn, stretch your left arm straight out. For a right turn, bend your left elbow so your hand points up. If you are going to stop, bend your left elbow so your hand points down.

Other safety tips for bikers are:
- Don't ride your bike on busy streets.
- Don't do stunts on your bike in the street.

- At night, wear light-colored clothing and reflectors.
- Watch out for loose rocks, sand, or anything that could make you lose control of the bike.
- Don't carry other people on your handlebars.

Seat belts in cars are an important safety feature. They keep your body in place. If you are not wearing a seat belt and the car stops suddenly, your body will keep moving forward and your head may hit the dashboard or windshield. You might even get thrown out of the car. A seat belt could save your life.

Buckle up! Wearing a seat belt can save your life.

Air bags for cars are tested on crash dummies.

Many cars have air bags. In an accident, air bags blow up like big balloons and protect the driver and passengers. Air bags have saved thousands of lives, but sometimes they can be dangerous. Air bags are released at a speed of 200 miles (322 kilometers) per hour. A child sitting in the front seat of a car can be killed when an air bag hits him or her. Experts say that children under the age of 12 should always sit in the backseat.

When you're riding in the family car, do you ever bug your brother or sister or your parents? That's not a good idea. Your parents need to pay attention to the road. They might get distracted if there's lot of arguing going on in the backseat or if they have to answer a lot of questions.

Can you imagine trying to drive a bus with twenty or more screaming kids? School bus drivers are responsible for many lives. Help the bus driver out by following a few safety rules.

- Stay in your seat.
- Don't throw things on the bus—or outside the bus.
- Never stick your arms out of the windows.
- Wait until the bus stops completely before you get off.

Too much racket can be distracting to the bus driver.

Safety at School

"Don't talk without raising your hand." "Wait in line." "Don't run in the hall." How many times have you heard a teacher say these things? Sometimes it seems like our whole lives are filled with rules. Would you like it better if there were no rules? Believe it or not, you wouldn't.

We need rules. Without them, life would be confusing. What if everybody talked at the same time in class? Nobody would be able to learn anything. How would you feel if other people cut in line right in front of you? That's why we have rules about waiting in line. Rules and laws help keep order and protect all of us.

Rules like raising your hand instead of shouting out help to give everyone a fair turn.

Rules help us learn to live together, but even rules can't make people get along with each other all the time. When you ride the school bus, is there a kid who always picks on you? When you walk down the hall, do some kids call you names or threaten to hurt you? A kid who picks on other kids, makes threats, or starts fights is a **bully**.

Bullies act really tough and mean to scare other kids. It makes them feel as though they are powerful. But the truth is, bullies are really cowards. They pick on other people so they can feel better about themselves. Most bullies scare and tease other people because they are scared. The kids they pick on are usually shy and sensitive. Bullies pick on kids who are not likely to fight back.

Does anyone pick on you? If so, play it cool and try to avoid a fight.

The best way to protect yourself against bullies is to have high **self-esteem**. Kids who feel good about themselves are less likely to get picked on. Bullies do not usually bother kids who stand up for themselves.

If a bully ever picks on you, do not react to the threats or name calling. The bully wants you to react. If a bully wants to fight and talking doesn't work, try to get away. There's no shame in avoiding a black eye or a bloody nose. Don't be afraid to tell your parents, your teachers, the principal, or any other adult. No one should have to put up with a bully!

Don't let a bully get to you. Talk to someone.

In recent years, violence in school has become a big problem. Some students threaten teachers and school officials. Some even bring knives, guns, and pipe bombs to school. How safe is your school?

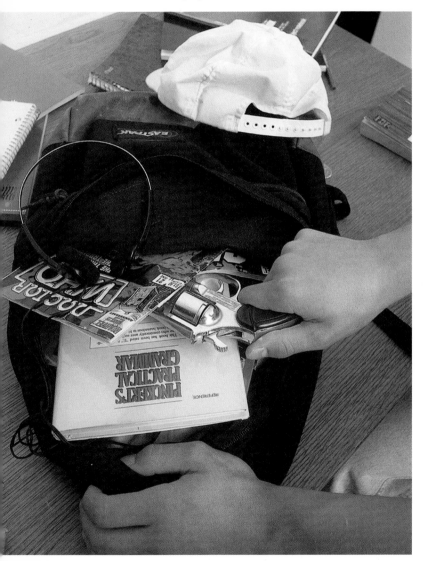

What can be done to protect students and teachers? Better gun control would help, but new gun laws may not be enough.

Adults who own guns must be responsible for them. Guns should be kept unloaded in a locked drawer or cabinet. The owner should carry the key and keep the gun and bullets in two different places. In some states, it is against the law to keep a loaded gun in a place where a child can get to it.

Guns don't belong in school.

Guns are only part of the problem, though. Some young people today feel that their troubles are more than they can handle. These children need support and understanding. They need someone to talk to—a parent, a teacher, a guidance counselor, or someone else who makes them comfortable. Kids who talk about their problems are less likely to act violently.

Talking to someone who listens can really make a difference.

If you have a friend who seems troubled, tell a responsible adult. If a friend has been talking about violence or brings a weapon to school, he or she needs more help than you can give. You're not tattling by asking an adult for help, you may actually be saving both your lives!

Safety with People

Since you were little, your parents have probably told you, "Don't talk to strangers." A stranger is a person you do not know. This includes the nicely dressed man who comes to your door, the teenage boy who delivers the morning newspaper, and the pretty lady at the checkout counter in the grocery store. It's okay if a stranger smiles at you and says hello. But if your parents are not with you, you should not talk to that person.

If there's a stranger at the door, call an adult.

Most strangers are nice people, but some are not. Bad strangers may try to hurt you. Unfortunately, you can't always tell the difference between good strangers and bad ones. That's why you need to beware of all strangers, no matter what they look like or how nice they may seem to be. If a stranger approaches you, keep the following tips in mind.

- Don't get too close to a stranger or a stranger's car. If you feel threatened, don't be afraid to draw attention to yourself. Yell!

- You don't have to answer a stranger's questions. Don't tell a stranger your name, your address, or what school you go to. Don't chat with strangers on the Internet.

- Don't take anything from a stranger. If a stranger offers you candy or toys, say "no" and walk away. Then tell your parents.

- Don't go anywhere with a stranger. Criminals may try to trick you. They may ask you to help carry a package or open a car door or find a lost dog. They may ask how to get to a certain place, and then say they need you to show them the way. Don't do it!

Criminals are less likely to approach kids who are in groups, so use the buddy system. When you walk to the store or the park, bring a friend or your brother or sister. Never walk alone.

It seems natural to kiss your parents goodnight or hug your best friend. We show affection in these ways. But sometimes it doesn't feel good to be touched. If someone touches you in a way that you don't like, it is called unwanted touching. Unwanted touching may involve hugging, pinching, tickling, kissing, or touching private parts. If you don't like they way someone touches you, speak up! Your body belongs to you.

If a stranger touches you on a crowded bus or train, move away quickly. Sometimes someone you know may touch you in a way you don't like. It's not easy to tell an aunt or an uncle or a sports coach that you don't like the way they touch you. You may be afraid you will hurt their feelings or spoil the relationship. There are several ways to deal with unwanted touching. Choose the ones that are right for you.

- If someone wants to hug you or kiss you, say you prefer to shake hands.
- If someone tries to pat your behind, tell the person to cut it out.
- If someone wants you to sit on his or her lap, just say, "No."
- If someone tries to touch your private parts or any other place that makes you uncomfortable, get away immediately.

If a person warns you not to tell about the touching or says, "It's our little secret," don't listen. Tell an adult you trust right away—a parent, a family friend, a teacher, or a guidance counselor.

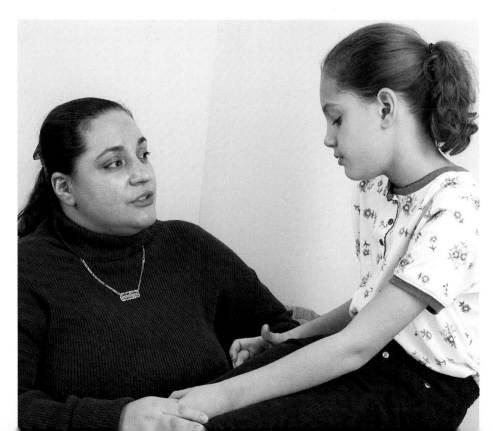

Don't keep problems bottled up inside. Talk to someone you trust.

What to Do in an Emergency?

It's a warm, sunny day. You and your friend are playing Frisbee. The Frisbee falls to the ground and your friend runs over to pick it up. When he reaches down, he cuts himself on some broken glass. His hand is bleeding. What do you do?

Most people hope they will never have to deal with an emergency, but it's always a good idea to be prepared.

Glass or sharp objects could be hiding in a leaf-covered lawn.

Keep Emergency Numbers on Hand

Be prepared for any emergency. Keep a list of important phone numbers next to the phone. Your address and phone number should be at the top of the list. When people get scared or upset, they may have trouble remembering their own home address when calling for help. Your emergency phone list should also include information for contacting 9-1-1 (for the fire department, police, or ambulance), your doctor's office, poison control, and a neighbor.

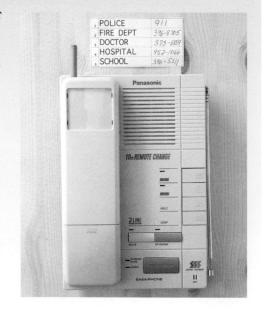

Keep emergency numbers next to the phone.

If someone is seriously hurt, get an adult right away and call an ambulance. For a serious injury, **first aid** can make a difference in a person's survival.

Is there a first-aid kit in your family's home and car? If not, help your parents make one. A first-aid kit should have bandages and supplies for treating cuts, insect bites, and other minor medical emergencies.

Here are the most important things to remember in case of an emergency: Stay calm, call for help, don't put yourself in danger, and don't move an injured person unless he or she is in immediate danger.

What to Do in an Emergency

Kind of Emergency	What to Do First	What to Do Next
Broken Bones	Call for help	Do not move the person unless he or she is in danger. Check for bleeding. Press a towel on any cuts until the bleeding stops.
Burns	Put the wound under cold water for at least 5 minutes.	Call the doctor if blisters form or if the skin is scorched
Cuts	Press a clean cloth on the wound to stop the bleeding. When it stops, wash the cut with soap and water, and put antibacterial ointment on it.	If the cut doesn't stop bleeding, call a doctor. For a nosebleed, hold your nose and look *down*, not up. If you hold your nose up, the blood can go into your throat and you may choke on it.
Electric shock from outlet	Don't touch the person.	Call for help. Use a wooden broom or a chair to push the person away from the outlet.
Fire in home	Get out of the house as fast as you can.	Call the fire department from a neighbor's house.
Insect sting	Call for help if the person is allergic to bee stings.	Run cold water on insect sting.
Poisoning	Take the "poison" away from the child.	Call poison control to find out what to do next.

Glossary

bully—someone who picks on others, making threats or acting violently

curcuit—the complete path that an electric current flows around

electricity—a current made up of charged particles

electric current—flowing electricity

first aid—emergency care for someone who is injured

flammable—something that can easily catch fire

melanin—a dark pigment in the skin

pedestrian—a person who is walking on the street

self-esteem—feeling good about oneself

tread water—to keep your head above water by pumping your legs up and down and moving your arms enough to keep you upright

ultraviolet ray—one of the powerful rays from the sun that can damage a person's skin

Learning More

Books

Boelts, Maribeth and Darwin. *Kids to the Rescue! First Aid Techniques for Kids*. Seattle, WA: Parenting Press, Inc., 1992.

Chaiet, Donna and Francine Russel. *The Safe Zone: A Kid's Guide to Personal Safety*. New York: Beech Tree, 1998.

A Child's First Library of Learning: Health & Safety. Alexandria, VA: Time-Life Books, Inc., 1996.

Kasdin, Karin and Laura Szabo-Cohen. *Disaster Blasters: A Kid's Guide to Being Home Alone*. New York: Avon Books, 1996.

Raatma, Lucia. *Safety at Home*. Mankato, MN: Bridgestone Books, 1999.

Online Sites

The Police Notebook: Kid Safety
http://www.ou.edu/oupd/kidsafe/kidmenu.htm
The University of Oklahoma Department of Public Safety provides information and animated pictures on topics such as avoiding fights, bullies, bus stop safety, electrical safety, emergencies, fires, home phone safety, what to do if you are lost, Internet safety, knives and guns, park safety, poison, stranger danger, and water safety.

Safety and Accident Prevention

http://www.amaassn.org/insight/h_focus/nemours/safety/index.htm

Information provided by the American Medical Association and the Nemours Foundation on topics including food safety, fire safety, rules for the car and school bus, playground safety, preventing sports injuries, and sun safety.

Super-Safe Kids Clubhouse

http://www.supersafekids.com/body_index.html

Meet animated characters like Nick 911, Safe-Place Sarah, No-Secrets Sam, and Rodney Rights and take an online quiz to see if you are a Super-Safe Kid.

Index

Page numbers in *italics* indicate illustrations.

About the Authors

Dr. Alvin Silverstein is a Professor of Biology at the College of Staten Island of the City University of New York. **Virginia Silverstein** is a translator of Russian scientific literature. The Silversteins first worked together on a research project at the University of Pennsylvania. Since then, they have produced 6 children and more than 150 published books for young people.

Laura Silverstein Nunn, a graduate of Kean College, has been helping with her parents' books since her high school days. She is the coauthor of more than twenty books on diseases and health, science concepts, endangered species, and pets. Laura lives with her husband Matt and their young son Cory in a rural New Jersey town not far from her childhood home.